Rosamund (Ball) Marriott Watson

The Bird-Bride

a Volume of Ballads and Sonnets

Rosamund (Ball) Marriott Watson

The Bird-Bride
a Volume of Ballads and Sonnets

ISBN/EAN: 9783743306134

Manufactured in Europe, USA, Canada, Australia, Japa

Cover: Foto ©ninafisch / pixelio.de

Manufactured and distributed by brebook publishing software
(www.brebook.com)

Rosamund (Ball) Marriott Watson

The Bird-Bride

CONTENTS

VERSES

TRANSLATIONS

NEW WORDS TO OLD TUNES

BALLAD OF THE BIRD-BRIDE

(*ESKIMO*)

THEY never come back, though I loved them well ;
  I watch the South in vain ;
The snow-bound skies are blear and grey,
Waste and wide is the wild gull's way,
  And she comes never again.

Years agone, on the flat white strand,
  I won my sweet sea-girl :
Wrapped in my coat of the snow-white fur,
I watched the wild birds settle and stir,
  The grey gulls gather and whirl.

One, the greatest of all the flock,
  Perched on an ice-floe bare,
Called and cried as her heart were broke,
And straight they were changed, that fleet bird-
    folk,
  To women young and fair.

7   B

Swift I sprang from my hiding-place
   And held the fairest fast;
I held her fast, the sweet, strange thing:
Her comrades skirled, but they all took wing,
   And smote me as they passed.

I bore her safe to my warm snow house;
   Full sweetly there she smiled;
And yet, whenever the shrill winds blew,
She would beat her long white arms anew,
   And her eyes glanced quick and wild.

But I took her to wife, and clothed her warm
   With skins of the gleaming seal;
Her wandering glances sank to rest
When she held a babe to her fair, warm breast,
   And she loved me dear and leal.

Together we tracked the fox and the seal,
   And at her behest I swore
That bird and beast my bow might slay
For meat and for raiment, day by day,
   But never a grey gull more.

A weariful watch I keep for aye
  'Mid the snow and the changeless frost :
Woe is me for my broken word !
Woe, woe's me for my bonny bird,
  My bird and the love-time lost !

Have ye forgotten the old keen life ?
  The hut with the skin-strewn floor ?
O winged white wife, and children three,
Is there no room left in your hearts for me,
  Or our home on the low sea-shore ?

Once the quarry was scarce and shy,
  Sharp hunger gnawed us sore,
My spoken oath was clean forgot,
My bow twanged thrice with a swift, straight shot,
  And slew me sea-gulls four.

The sun hung red on the sky's dull breast,
  The snow was wet and red ;
Her voice shrilled out in a woful cry,
She beat her long white arms on high,
  ' The hour is here,' she said.

She beat her arms, and she cried full fain
　　As she swayed and wavered there.
' Fetch me the feathers, my children three,
Feathers and plumes for you and me,
　　Bonny grey wings to wear ! '

They ran to her side, our children three,
　　With the plumage black and grey ;
Then she bent her down and drew them near,
She laid the plumes on our children dear,
　　'Mid the snow and the salt sea-spray.

' Babes of mine, of the wild wind's kin,
　　Feather ye quick, nor stay.
Oh, oho ! but the wild winds blow !
Babes of mine, it is time to go :
　　Up, dear hearts, and away ! '

And lo ! the grey plumes covered them all,
　　Shoulder and breast and brow.
I felt the wind of their whirling flight :
Was it sea or sky ? was it day or night ?
　　It is always night-time now.

Dear, will you never relent, come back ?
  I loved you long and true.
O winged white wife, and our children three,
Of the wild wind's kin though ye surely be,
  Are ye not of my kin too ?

Ay, ye once were mine, and, till I forget,
  Ye are mine forever and aye,
Mine, wherever your wild wings go,
While shrill winds whistle across the snow
  And the skies are blear and grey.

BALLAD OF PENTYRE TOWN

(CORNISH)

TO E. A. S.

FOAM flies white over rocks of black,
  Nights are dark when the boats go down ;
But souls flit back in the wild wind's track,
  And grey gulls gather in Pentyre Town.

Wild, grey gulls in the narrow street,
  Wheeling, wavering, to and fro,
(Dear the echo of banished feet !)
  Flocking in as the sun sinks low.

Pale she stands at her open door,
  (Dark little streets of a fishing town ;)
Shrill, thin voices from sea and shore
  Fill the air as the sun goes down.

'Out and alas for my woe !' saith she,
  (See how the grey gulls whirl and throng !)
'Love ! Come back from the weary sea !'
  (Sore is sorrow and hours are long.)

One comes sailing with outstretched beak,
  White throat lifted in wailing cry,
Stoops his wing to a woman's cheek,
  Swift and light, as he wavers by.

Foam flies white over rocks of black,
  Nights are dark when the boats go down ;
But souls flit back in the wild wind's track,
  And grey gulls gather in Pentyre Town.

Still she stands at her open door,
  (Flickering sun rays faint and far,)
'Woe is heavy and doubt is sore,'
  (Sobbing waves on the dull Doom Bar.)

'Sleep flees far from mine eyes,' saith she,
  (Skies are wild with the rough wind's breath,)
'All for my love's voice calling me,'
  (Robbed Love clings at the knees of Death.)

Now she strays on the wind-swept strand,
  'Fair our wandering days shall be !'
Sets her foot on the wan wet sand,
  (Faint feet falter, but wings flash free.)

BALLAD OF PENTYRE TOWN

'Love, I come to your call at last.'
  (Black boats lean on the low seashore.)
'Fear and doubting are overpast,'
  (Set the tiller, and grasp the oar !)

No boat stirs on the sea's dark breast,
  (Long clouds writhe on a pallid sky,)
Storm-winds wail to the lurid West,
  Sad and shrill as a seabird's cry.

Foam flies white over rocks of black,
  Daylight dies, and a boat goes down ;
But souls flit back in the wild wind's track,
  And grey gulls gather in Pentyre Town.

LE MAUVAIS LARRON

(SUGGESTED BY WILLETTE'S PICTURE)

THE moorland waste lay hushed in the dusk of the
    second day,
Till a shuddering wind and shrill moaned up through
    the twilight grey ;
Like a wakening wraith it rose from the grave of the
    buried sun,
And it whirled the sand by the tree—(there was
    never a tree but one—)
But the tall bare bole stood fast, unswayed with the
    mad wind's stress,
And a strong man hung thereon in his pain and his
    nakedness.
His feet were nailed to the wood, and his arms
    strained over his head ;
'Twas the dusk of the second day, and yet was the
    man not dead.

The cold blast lifted his hair, but his limbs were set
    and stark,
And under their heavy brows his eyes stared into the
    dark :
He looked out over the waste, and his eyes were as
    coals of fire,
Lit up with anguish and hate, and the flame of a
    strong desire.

The dark blood sprang from his wounds, the cold
    sweat stood on his face,
For over the darkening plain came a rider riding
    apace.
Her rags flapped loose in the wind ; the last of the
    sunset glare
Flung dusky gold on her brow and her bosom broad
    and bare.
She was haggard with want and woe, on a jaded
    steed astride,
And still, as it staggered and strove, she smote on its
    heaving side,
Till she came to the limbless tree where the tortured
    man hung high—
A motionless crooked mass on a yellow streak in the
    sky.

''Tis I—I am here, Antoine—I have found thee at
last,' she said ;

'O the hours have been long, but long ! and the
minutes as drops of lead.

Have they trapped thee, the full-fed flock, thou wert
wont to harry and spoil ?

Do they laugh in their town secure o'er their measures
of wine and oil ?

Ah God ! that these hands might reach where they
loll in their rich array ;

Ah God, that they were but mine, all mine, to mangle
and slay !

How they shuddered and shrank, erewhile, at the
sound of thy very name,

When we lived as the grey wolves live, whom torture
nor want may tame :

And thou but a man ! and still a scourge and a
terror to men,

Yet only my lover to me, my dear, in the rare days
then.

O years of revel and love ! ye are gone as the wind
goes by,

He is snared and shorn of his strength, and the
anguish of hell have I—

I am here, O love, at thy feet; I have ridden far and
   fast
To gaze in thine eyes again, and to kiss thy lips at
   the last.'
She rose to her feet and stood upright on the gaunt
   mare's back,
And she pressed her full red lips to his that were
   strained and black.
'Good-night, for the last time now—good-night,
   beloved, and good-bye—'
And his soul fled into the waste between a kiss and
   a sigh.

DEID FOLKS' FERRY

'TIS They, of a veritie—
  They are calling thin an' shrill ;
We maun rise an' put to sea,
  We maun gi'e the deid their will,
We maun ferry them owre the faem,
  For they draw us as they list ;
We maun bear the deid folk hame
  Through the mirk an' the saft sea-mist.

' But how can I gang the nicht,
  When I'm new come hame frae sea ?
When my heart is sair for the sicht
  O' my lass that langs for me ? '
' O your lassie lies asleep,
  An' sae do your bairnies twa ;
The cliff-path's stey an' steep,
  An' the deid folk cry an' ca'.'

O sae hooly steppit we,
   For the nicht was mirk an' lown,
Wi' never a sign to see,
   But the voices all aroun'.
We laid to the saut sea-shore,
   An' the boat dipped low i' th' tide,
As she micht hae dipped wi' a score,
   An' our ain three sel's beside.

O the boat she settled low,
   Till her gunwale kissed the faem,
An' she didna loup nor row
   As she bare the deid folk hame ;
But she aye gaed swift an' licht,
   An' we naething saw nor wist
Wha sailed i' th' boat that nicht
   Through the mirk an' the saft sea-mist.

There was never a sign to see,
   But a misty shore an' low ;
Never a word spak' we,
   But the boat she lichtened slow,

An' a cauld sigh stirred my hair,
  An' a cauld hand touched my wrist,
An' my heart sank cauld an' sair
  I' the mirk an' the saft sea-mist.

Then the wind raise up wi' a maen,
  ('Twas a waefu' wind, an' weet),
Like a deid saul wud wi' pain,
  Like a bairnie wild wi' freit ;
But the boat rade swift an' licht,
  Sae we wan the land fu' sune,
An' the shore showed wan an' white
  By a glint o' the waning mune.

We steppit oot owre the sand
  Where an unco' tide had been,
An' Black Donald caught my hand
  An' coverit up his een :
For there, in the wind an' weet,
  Or ever I saw nor wist,
My Jean an' her weans lay cauld at my feet,
  In the mirk an' the saft sea-mist.

An' it's O for my bonny Jean!
     An' it's O for my bairnies twa,
It's O an' O for the watchet een
     An' the steps that are gane awa'—
Awa' to the Silent Place,
     Or ever I saw nor wist,
Though I wot we twa went face to face
     Through the mirk an' the saft sea-mist.

THE CRUEL PRIEST

IT was at the court o' the gude Scots King
  That a waefu' thing befell :
'Tis of a lover and his lady ;
  Loved ilk the other well.

There cam' a lord frae the South Countrie,
  And a gudely lord was he ;
His sword-sheath was o' the beaten gowd,
  The haft o' the ivory.

And aye he spak' o' his gowd and gear,
  And his lands in the South Countrie,
But never he spak' o' his faith and troth,
  That were plight to a fair lady.

Oh, then was our gude King right fain :
  ' In a gude time cam' he here ;
Braid lands hath he in the South Countrie—
  He shall wed my daughter dear ! '

He's called to him his little foot-page;
  'Gae rin, gae rin,' quoth he,
'And see that ye carry this braid letter
  To the lord frae the South Countrie!'

Then up and spak' the Southland lord—
  And oh, but his cheek waxed red—
'Oh, I wadna wed the King's daughter
  Though a' but her were dead!

'Gae back, gae back to your King,' he said,
  'And this word gie frae me:
My heart and my hand are no my ain,
  Nor yet for that fair lady.'

Then back cam' he, that little foot-page,
  And knelt down on his knee:
'Oh, will ye wed wi' the King's daughter,
  Or will ye be hangit hie?'

'Oh, where, oh, where is my gude grey steed?
  Oh, where are my merry men a'?
Oh, would I were far frae this ill countrie,
  At hame in my father's ha'!

'But gin I maun wed this outland maid
   An ill death may she die!
She may ware her love on him she will;
   She's get nae love frae me.'

Then bells were rung and mass was sung,
   And ready stude the priest,
But deid in her bower lay the King's daughter,
   With a wide wound in her breist!

Then a wofu' man was our gude King,
   And the saut tear filled his ee:
'Now streak the corp, ye Four Maries,[1]
   And busk her in cramoisie.

'And you that wished my daughter dead
   Your bridal yet shall be.
This very night ye's be wed,' he said,
   'And the morn ye's be hangit hie!'

.   .   .   .   .   .

---

[1] Four Maries. This title for a lady's waiting-woman is by no
means confined, in the ballads, to Mary Seton, Mary Beatton, Mary
Carmichael, and Mary Hamilton, the ladies of Mary Stuart.

Then by cam' the bride's company
    Wi' torches burning bright.
'Tak' up, tak' up your bonny bride
    A' in the mirk midnight!'

Oh, wan, wan was the bridegroom's face
    And wan, wan was the bride,
But clay-cauld was the young mess priest
    That stood them twa beside!

Says, 'Rax me out your hand, Sir Knight,
    And wed her wi' this ring;'
And the deid bride's hand it was as cauld
    As ony earthly thing.

The priest he touched that lady's hand,
    And never a word he said;
The priest he touched that lady's hand,
    And his ain was wet and red.

The priest he lifted his ain right hand,
    And the red blood dripped and fell.
Says, 'I loved ye, lady, and ye loved me:
    Sae I took your life mysel'.'

Oh! red, red was the dawn o' day,
  And tall was the gallows-tree :
The Southland lord to his ain has fled
  And the mess-priest's hangit hie!

FRAGMENT OF THE 'FAUSE BRITHER'

O the win' blaws thro' my [ling long] hair,
　An' the rain draps owre my bree ;
I've crossed the seas to my ain luve's bouir,
　An' she winna speak wi' me.
　　.　　.　　.　　.　　.　　.

Gin ye be her true luve Willie,
　As weel I wot ye be,
Gae speir at the worms i' yon kirkyard
　[They'se aiblins crack wi' ye].

He's turn'd him frae his ain luve's bouir
　Wi' the saut tear in his ee,
An' he's awa' to the cauld kirkyard
　As fast as he can [flee].

O what's come o' your bonny een,
　That were sae braw [and bright] ?
An' what's come o' your sma' fingers,
　That were sae lang an' white ?

O my bonny een are gane, Willie,
　　But and my fingers sma',
An' the gowden ring ye gie'd to me
　　Is tint [and wede awa'].

O haud your tongue o' your weeping, Willie,
　　For ye've been ower lang owre sea ;
I canna sleep [for the wound sae deep]
　　My brither gie'd to me.

THE BLIND GHOST

'TIS a marshy land and low,
　This place where the dead folk be,
And, aye, as they come and go,
　They shoulder and jostle me.

I feel the birds flit by,
　On their soft wings flapping free,—
But groping and slow go I,
　Who am blind and cannot see.

And whenever the boat comes in,
　And her keel bites on the strand,
With a wavering, whispering din
　The cold wraiths flock to land.

Then I rise and I grope along
　To the soft dank landing-place,
Where the voices thickest throng,
　And the blown spray wets my face.

The cold wraiths rustle anigh—
　'Art thou come?—I am waiting yet—
I am here! do not pass me by—
　I am here, May-Margaret!'

Oh, 'tis hard, and so hard to hear!
　For the many voices round,
That wrangle, and weep, and jeer,
　While the full barge grates aground.

Oh, I hold my breath to hear,
　While the sobs rise in my throat,
And my heart throbs thick with fear
　Lest she lighten from the boat,—

And I hear her not—but bide,
　When her steps are passed and gone,
By the weary water-side,
　Aye hearkening—aye alone.

Still they clamour and jostle me,
　Still the boat fares to and fro,
And the face I may never see,
　Ah, God! that my heart may know!

KING SOLOMON'S DREAM

BETWEEN the darkness and the dawn
  Three signs were seen of me :
One, white as ivory new-sawn,
And greener one than wet spring grass
And one, more red than blood (alas !
  No sadder sight may be) ;
    All these things verily
    Mine eyes did see.

Three ladies in a twilight space
  Did sit and spin alway :
The first, a damsel cold of grace,
With snow-white spindle featly wove ;
The second (singing low of love),
  With spindle green as bay,
    Smiled soft and looked on me—
    Yea—even she.

But that third lady of the three,
   I might not see her face,
Or whether fair or foul was she,
For veils wound close about her head
(Both veil and spindle were blood-red);
    And still she span apace,
      Singing right joylessly,
      Nor looked on me.

The first I spake with of the three,
   The virgin pure and pale,
Full fair and exquisite to see,
More delicate than spring sunlight,
Crowned with closed buds of lilies white
    And swathed in pearl-white veil.—
      Sweet lady, even she
      Did answer me!

'When Eve, in woe and sorrow sore,
   Came forth from Paradise,
The dear-bought bough her hand still bore :
She had no carven coffer fair,
Nor ivory chest, to lay it there :

The tears from her sweet eyes
   Did fall to water it,
   As was most fit.

' She said, " Alas ! this goodly bough
   Hath cost me grievous woe ;
Yet must I guard it even now ;
Yea, surely will I plant it here."—
Full fast the tree grew (bought so dear !)
   Right large, and white as snow ;
     A token stood the tree
     Of Eve's virginity.'

The maiden ceased, and turned her head ;
   No word she spake again.
The second, fair with white and red,
And loose hair crowned with clustering vine,
Did turn her lustrous eyes on mine.—
   ' But I of Love's great gain,'
     She said, ' of Love and Pain
     Sing, not in vain.

' Above, the snow-white branches spread ;
   Below, the dewy grass—
In sooth a goodly bridal-bed—

And then the tree waxed great and green
With broad, fair leaves of glossy sheen ;
   And there it came to pass
     That Eve, in travail sore,
     Prince Abel bore.'

The third dame cried, ' Ah, bitter woe ! '—
   Full sore a little space
She wrung her hands, then, moaning low,
She said, ' Blood-red the tall tree grew
Whenso Prince Cain his brother slew :
   Mild Abel, fair of face,
     Where first he drew soft breath
     Received the death.'

She ceased, and fell to sorrowing ;
   Then I—' Still sorrow ye ? '
Her speech broke forth again, ' O King,
In your fair garden straightly set,
That wondrous tree is growing yet.'—
   ' And still shall these things be ? '
     ' Even so,' she answered me,
     ' Yea, verily.'

THE FAIRIES' COBBLER

I SAT at work 'neath the lintel low,
  And the white-walled street was still,
Save for the sound of my neighbour's loom,
'*Plik-a-plek-plek*,' through the twilight gloom,
  And a curlew crying shrill.

The curlew cried, and I raised my head,
  For I felt the good folk near ;
Slim little shapes in the fading light,
Dusk and dim, but their eyes gleamed bright,
  And they hailed me thin and clear.

In they swept with a rustling sound,
  Like dead leaves blown together ;
Bade me fashion their dainty shoon,
'O the morrow's e'en is the Feast o' the Moon,
  And we dance on the rare white heather !'

So I took their gay stuffs, woven well,
   As never a mortal weaves ;
Fashioned daintily, fashioned fair,
Little red shoon that the Pixies wear,
   Of the blood-red autumn leaves.

They stood at my knee, they crowded near,
   And shrilled a piping tune,
Their great eyes glowed, and they whispered
     'Quick!'
And my work went merrily, 'tic-tac-tic,'
   By the light of the yellow moon.

'Thanks and thanks for thy labour done,
   And aye when the summer's o'er,
And reapers carry the last brown sheaf,
We'll send our sign of a yellow leaf,
   A leaf blown in at the door.

'So shall ye know that the time hath come,
   And merry at heart shall rise,
Rise and go where we flit and fleet,
Follow the track of our twinkling feet
   And the glow of our golden eyes.'

They reeled away through the starlight air
   And cried, 'On our crystal shore,
O Friend, you shall 'scape the winter's grief :
Follow the sign of the yellow leaf,
   The leaf blown in at the door !'

So shall I know when the time hath come,
   And merry at heart shall rise,
Rise and go where they flit and fleet,
The little red shoon on the twinkling feet
   And the glow of the golden eyes.

Winter will come with snow-stilled skies,
   And the neighbours' hearths aglow ;
But the owls will drowse on my cold hearth-stone,
For I shall be gone where the birds are flown
   And the great moon-daisies blow.

I sit at work 'neath the lintel low,
   And the white-walled street is still ;
The twilight deepens dim and grey :
To-morrow it may be—not to-day—
   And I wait the Pixies' will.

MÄRCHEN

A FERLIE cam' ben to me yestreen,
  A lady jimp an' sma',
Wi' a milk-white snood an' a kirtle green ;
Yellow an' bricht were her bonny een,
  An' she said, ' Will ye come awa' ?

' Will ye gang wi' me to the Elfin knowe
  To milk our Queenie's coo ? '
' Na, na,' quo' I, ' I maun shear my sheep ;
I've my barn to bigg an' my corn to reap,
  Sae I canna come the noo.'

The ferlie skirled as she turned to gae,
  For an angry elf was she,
' O a wilfu' man maun hae his way,
An' I mak' sma' doot but ye'se rue the day
  That ye wouldna gang wi' me.'

D

'O once again will ye speir at me,
  An' I'll aiblins come awa'?'
'O I'll come again to your yetts,' quo' she,
'When broom blaws bricht on yon rowan tree
  An' the laverock sings i' th' snaw.'

SONNETS

AN INTERLUDE

SIGHING she spoke, and leaning clasped her knees :—
  ' Well hast thou sung of living men and dead,
    Of fair deeds done, and far lands visited.
Sing now of things more marvellous than these !
Of fruits ungathered on unplanted trees,
    Of songs unsung, of gracious words unsaid,
    Of that dim shore where no man's foot may tread,
Of strangest skies, and unbeholden seas !

' Full many a golden web our longings spin,
    And days are fair, and sleep is over-sweet ;
    But passing sweet those moments rare and fleet,
When red spring sunlight, tremulous and thin,
    Makes quick the pulses with tumultuous beat
For meadows never won, or wandered in.'

OMAR KHAYYÁM

TO A. L.

SAYER of sooth, and Searcher of dim skies!
  Lover of Song, and Sun, and Summertide,
  For whom so many roses bloomed and died ;
Tender Interpreter, most sadly wise,
Of earth's dumb, inarticulated cries !
  Time's self cannot estrange us, nor divide ;
  Thy hand still beckons from the garden-side,
Through green vine-garlands, when the Winter dies.

Thy calm lips smile on us, thine eyes are wet ;
  The nightingale's full song sobs all through thine,
  And thine in hers,—part human, part divine !
Among the deathless gods thy place is set,
  All-wise, but drowsy with Life's mingled Wine,
Laughter and Learning, Passion and Regret.

TO HERODOTUS

FAR-TRAVELLED coaster of the midland seas,
  What marvels did those curious eyes behold !—
  Winged snakes, and carven labyrinths of old ;
The emerald column raised to Heracles ;
King Perseus' shrine upon the Chemmian leas ;
  Four-footed fishes, decked with gems and gold :
  But thou didst leave some secrets yet untold,
And veiled the dread Osirian mysteries.

And now the golden asphodels among
  Thy footsteps fare, and to the lordly dead
  Thou tellest all the stories left unsaid
Of secret rites and runes forgotten long,
  Of that dark folk who ate the Lotus-bread
And sang the melancholy Linus-song.

BOCCACCIO

Now let yon idle tales forgotten be
  (Forsaken follies of a fervid youth),
  And set on high my strivings after truth ;
Lest women young and fair cry shame on me,
Saying, 'for sure a graceless knave was he,
  Some lewd light jongleur of the drinking-booth.'

  .   .   .   .

In vain, Boccaccio ; these are dead, in sooth—
And those, foredoomed to immortality.

But we forgive thy ribaldries, for, hark !
  Pure Lisa sighs the olive-groves among ;
  We see Simona smiling, venom-stung,
Sylvestra's lover lying cold and stark ;—
  Death from thy viol noble songs hath wrung,
As nightingales sing loudest in the dark.

BOUCHER

'LEAD me this evening to my painter's chair'
  (Dying, he said); 'lay here upon my knee
  The palette—now the pencils give to me,
And set my Venus on the easel there,
So that the sunlight gleams upon her hair
  And her white body, risen from the sea :
  Leave us—alone awhile we twain would be ;
I who must die, and she for ever fair.'

Above the flocking Loves, the sea's blue rim,
  A shadow followed as the sun-rays fled ;
  Grey, up the ivory breast, the golden head,
It stole ; but, steadfast through the twilight dim,
  Still on his idol gazed the sightless dead,
And still the rose-crowned goddess smiled on him.

DEATH AND JUSTICE

DEATH doth not claim us with the passing breath ;
  Before our Lady Justice calm he stands,
  To hear her grave, immutable commands.
' Wait, I shall tell you presently,' she saith ;
' Wait but a moment's space, my brother, Death,
  While Time, our kinsman, shakes his silent sands.'
  She holds the balance true, with steady hands
And strong, the little while it wavereth.

Hatred and Envy must lie still and wait ;
  So, now, must Love and Sorrow stand aside
  In breathless silence, pale and eager-eyed,
Till, through the lips of Justice, speaketh Fate,—
  ' Death, in thy keeping must the man abide ;
Or, ' He shall live for aye—his work is great.'

AN UNBIDDEN GUEST

I SAID, my dwelling-place is passing fair,
  My dusk, dim chamber where the daylight dies :
  No sun doth blind, no tears may vex mine eyes ;
Cast out alike are Glory and Despair.
My soul is banishèd—I wot not where.
  I thrust him forth, unheedful of his cries,
  Long years ago : full vain is thine emprise,
O shrouded Stranger from the outer air !

He smiles, a bitter merriment is his !
  His footsteps falter not, but still draw nigh ;
  He holds a crystal cresset-flame on high.
' So, friend, at last we meet again—is *this*
  The home forbidden me in years gone by ?
Behold, how desolate and bare it is ! '

FULFILMENT

FULFILMENT mocks at Hope's foreshadowing,
  On ruined fruits her sullen lips are fed ;
  Athwart the last-limned dream, the song last said,
She sweeps the leaden shadow of her wing,
A bitter burden of bare blight to bring,
  In sudden disenchantment, dull and dead.
  And so we waken—in our seraph's stead
To find a gaping goblin-changeling.

Sweet Hope is slain, come let us bury her ;
  The dream is done, the labour lost, we say ;
  But ofttimes, gazing on the lifeless clay,
The old fire fills our veins, our longings stir ;
  And still, to strive anew, we turn away
From yet another dead Hope's sepulchre.

COMPENSATION

IF Joy and Perfectness have crowned a day,
  Alas! we say, This gracious day is done ;
  The gods will never send us such an one
Again, however we may strive and pray.
But if in woe that knoweth no allay
  Full slow the anguish-harrowed hours have run,
  Our hearts grow lighter with the setting sun,
For then we feel that all hours pass away.

Now some are bound to Life with golden bands,
  And Life to these is passing sweet and dear ;
  They fain would linger in each lovely year
And shun the pilgrimage to unknown lands.
  But souls that sorrow know not any fear
When Death draws nigh with healing in his hands.

TO-DAY

TO A. G. T.

I.

CLASP close my hand ; this little space is ours,
 This safe green shore between two bitter seas,
 A narrow meadow-land of love and ease,
Made musical with birds and fair with flowers.
For all the fragrance of the rose-hung bowers,
 For all the shelter of the dusky trees,
 We thank thee, Fortune ! Yea, upon our knees,
With tears we praise thee for these perfect hours.

Look not where Yesterday's dull current laves
 The misty sea-board of our landing-place—
 Clasp close my hand, and turn to me thy face,
Before we tempt To-morrow's tossing waves :
 Forget, in this dear moment's certain grace,
That Time and Fate press on—and hold us slaves.

TO-NIGHT

II.

ALAS! my heart shrinks chill before To-night;
  The birds keep silence now; the air is grey
  And salt with leaping foam of Yesterday,
Lashed into fury with the shrill wind's flight.
To-day hath shrunk too narrow for delight:
  To-morrow's billows raven for their prey;
  Through gathering dusk, low-gleaming on its way,
The rolling tide advances, wild and white.

Thy mournful face is fading from my sight,
  Though still thy hand clings steadfastly in mine;
  The dawn draws near to bid us both resign
Our storm-worn shallop to the tide-wave's might:
  Yet this, a little while, was mine and thine—
One green vine-garland plucked in Fate's despite.

LAST YEAR'S LEAVES

THE clear-eyed Spring flits by in fitful wise
    With whistling winds, and sun-gifts scantly spread ;
    Yet new growths venture in the dead blooms' stead,
And, sweetly shrill, brown bird to bird replies.
Still wearing something of last summer's guise,
    Some few faint leaves the branches have not shed
    Drop, dimly green, while others burn blood-red
Between the thin spring sunlight and mine eyes.

Old pains, old pleasures, these have had their day,
    And strong new hopes and dreams are bourgeoning.
    What though, a little space, the old thoughts cling ?
The young shoots blindly push their sturdy way
    When green sap quickens in the veins of spring ;
But last year's leaves hang loose upon the spray.

AT EVENING

How will it fare with us when we are old ?
  Shall we, through gathering greyness and dull rain,
  Grieve that the red leaves fall and blossoms wane ?
Shall we, indeed, through mists of time behold
Our youth's lost picture limned on gleaming gold ?
  Ah, no—well gone is all past joy and pain—
  No more, for April hours and fancies fain,
Our souls shall crave dead dreams and tales untold.

If we could choose what boon the years might bring,
  Should we not ask that age might proffer peace ?
No more the doubt and deep unrest of Spring ;
But woods unstirred by wind of wavering wing,
  The quietude of grey untroubled seas,
And still green meadows hushed at evening.

E

MOONRISE

ADOWN the dim green glen beside the deep,
　　Along the hollow hill-slopes wet with dew,
　　Like phantoms flocking in the twilight blue,
Home from their pastures troop the drowsy sheep ;
Slow-dying sun-rays dream upon the steep,
　　And, heralded by bird-notes faint and few,
　　Peace, with night's dusky dawn, is born anew
While sea-winds sing of solitude and sleep.

The full moon rises round and rosy-red
　　Behind the grass-grown shoulder of the hill ;
　　Naught now remains to sigh for or fulfil—
The sunset fades, and life lies perfected
　　This little space, while, dreamy-slow and still,
Sweet Evening stoops to crown Day's weary head.

AN AUTUMN MORNING

A SUNNY autumn morning, calm and stilled,
   Smiles on the bare, burnt meadows ; down the lane
   The hedge-fruits ripen, fresh with last night's rain,
Among broad leaves the sun begins to gild ;
The crisp low-breathing air no frost has chilled,
   Sweet with pine-fragrance, stings the sense again,
   With joy so keen it meets the lips of pain
With dim desires and fancies unfulfilled.

Ah, swift and sudden as a swallow's flight
   These flitting golden glimpses come and go ;
   The Unseen clasps us through the veil, and, lo !
Our blood stirs strangely with a deep delight—
Old dreams, vague visions, glimmer on our sight,
   All we have known, and all we may not know.

SOIR D'AUTOMNE

(AFTER CABANEL)

HERE, where the fading sunset bathes my face,
  Hold thou my hand the while I lean on thee.
  The dying leaves hang loose upon the tree ;
Soft broods the autumn evening's languid grace.
With slow step stealing from our resting-place,
  Our Past, departing, waves his hand to me :
  With dim, veiled brow he goes : reluctantly
He turns him from us at the low hill's base.

So sweet, so sad, so still, this silent hour ;
  My heart throbs slow in solemn ecstasy :
  The golden air is faint with memory,
And gracious weariness is evening's dower.
  Fled is our summer ; but a little while
  Is left us yet the mellow sunset smile.

BLIND MAN'S HOLIDAY

WHEN vanished is the gold and violet,
   And all the pearl and opal turned to grey,
   We call the drowsy children from their play.
'Come, bonny birds, to roost ; the sun has set !'
And still they cry, 'We are not sleepy yet ;
   Only a little longer may we stay—
   Only a little while ? ' half-sighing say ;
'We were so still, we hoped you might forget.'

We, too, delay, with childish stratagem,
   The while we break our playthings one by one,
Sobbing our foolish hearts out over them ;
   Till comes the wise nurse Death, at set of sun,
   When, wearied out and piteous, we run
Weeping to her and clasp her garments' hem.

TIME

THEY err who picture Time outworn and old ;
  A youth for ever blithe and fair he stands,
  Wasting our days with swift destructive hands,
Freezing our lives with careless eyes and cold :
Lost is all wealth whereon he taketh hold,
  And none gainsay or cancel his commands,
  So stern his lips ! though wreathed with ruddy
      strands
Of rose and poppy gleam his locks of gold.

He flings the drooping garlands from his hair,
  And others frail and fresh he gathereth ;
Smiling, he mocks our love and our despair ;
  Heedless, he guides us to the Gates of Death,
  And ' Here the ways divide for aye,' he saith—
' Farewell,' he saith, and passeth unaware.

HEREAFTER

SHALL we not weary in the windless days
   Hereafter, for the murmur of the sea,
   The cool salt air across some grassy lea ?
Shall we not go bewildered through a maze
Of stately streets with glittering gems ablaze,
   Forlorn amid the pearl and ivory,
   Straining our eyes beyond the bourne to see
Phantoms from out Life's dear, forsaken ways ?

Give us again the crazy clay-built nest,
   Summer, and soft unseasonable spring,
   Our flowers to pluck, our broken songs to sing,
Our fairy gold of evening in the West ;
   Still to the land we love our longings cling,
The sweet, vain world of turmoil and unrest.

VERSES

THE FAIRIES' VALEDICTION

HEAR them cry 'Good-night! Good-bye!'
Piping voices sweet and shrill
Pierce the dusk from hill to hill.
'We are weary of you all,
High and humble, great and small.
Mortal anguish, mortal rage,
We will never more assuage;
Mortal pleasures, mortal pain,
Never will behold again.

'Once we loved your short-lived race,
Once we found you fair of face:
Smiled on golden lad and lass,
Brought their happiness to pass.
But your spring is all too brief,
Wrinkled as an autumn leaf;
Laidly as a goblin jest
Wax your loveliest and best—

Withered lips and faded eyes,
Lips unfit for lovers' sighs,
Eyes that may no more behold
Moonlight magic, elfin gold.

' Then, like drowsy moles, you creep
In the Earth-king's realm to sleep ;
Leave the sun, that loved you well,
With the dark Dwarf-folk to dwell.
Those that hymned us worthily,
Even them we may not free !

' Hidden from your clouded eyes
Still we ride the dragon-flies ;
Tho' we sing, no earthly ear
Now our twilight songs may hear ;
Tho' we whirl the withered leaves,
Skim above the harvest sheaves,
Smooth greensward, or amber shore,
You shall see us never more—
Never more by sea or sky !
Good-night, Good-by ! '

BIRDS OF PASSAGE

(' *A LOST CHANCE FLIES OWRE THE SEA* ')

' TURN, turn again ! ' we call, and all in vain,
' Birds light of wing, that waver over-sea,
That lit erewhile, when blind, alas ! were we ;
Now we behold your breasts of bronze and gold,
Swift sapphire wings, and bills of ivory.'

They waver by, they gleam 'tween sea and sky ;
Turn, bonny birds—oh ! turn ye to the shore,
And glorify our hovels mean and poor ;
Make sweet of cheer our wattled houses here,
Build 'neath the eaves, nor leave us ever more.'

Afar they swing, on soft relentless wing ;
They seek the Sunset Islands of the West,
The mellow low-lit meadows of the Blest,
Where poplars grey for ever sigh and sway,
And all desires and dreams are laid to rest.

ARSINOË'S CATS

Imitation of the manner of the later Greek poets, circ. A.D. 500.   Cats
were unknown in historic Greece till about the Christian era.

ARSINOË the fair, the amber-tressed,
   Is mine no more ;
Cold as the unsunned snows are is her breast,
   And closed her door.
No more her ivory feet and tresses braided
   Make glad mine eyes ;
Snapt are my viol-strings, my flowers are faded—
   My love-lamp dies.

Yet, once, for dewy myrtle-buds and roses,
   All summer long,
We searched the twilight-haunted garden closes
   With jest and song.
Ay, all is over now—my heart hath changèd
   Its heaven for hell ;
And that ill chance which all our love estrangèd
   In this wise fell :

A little lion, small and dainty sweet
  (For such there be !),
With sea-grey eyes and softly-stepping feet,
  She prayed of me.
For this, through lands Egyptian far away
  She bade me pass ;
But in an evil hour, I said her nay—
  And now, alas !
Far-travelled Nicias hath wooed and won
  Arsinoë
With gifts of furry creatures white and dun
  From over-sea.

A PORTRAIT

THERE, my ingle-nook above,
See the Lady of my Love,
  Standing there
With her dainty, sandalled feet,
Limp, high-waisted gown, and sweet
  Curling hair.

Deep her eyes, and pale her check,
(Oft I wonder—could she speak—
  Were it best?)
Faintly smiling, still she stands,
Yellow roses in her hands—
  On her breast.

And the glory of her prime
Neither tears nor tyrant time
  May impair;

All the changing seasons through
I can still believe her true,
 Think her fair.

Mute for her are praise and blame,
For my gracious Lady's name
 No one knows ;
Nor, for treasure-bags untold,
Would I hearken how the old
 Story goes.

Though the fallen embers fill
Half the hearth with ashes chill,
 Soft and grey,
Never lonely or forlorn
Will she leave me, nor in scorn
 Turn away.

You will never leave my home,
You will never change, nor roam,
 O my Dear!
And your roses fill the room
With their freshness and perfume
 All the year.

F

Dame and flowers were dead, I know—
Just a century ago,
   To a day!
Yet, dear Lady, I maintain
In my love you live again,
   Mine for aye.

A SILHOUETTE

THERE hangs her graceful silhouette
(A cameo, as it were, of jet),
Mine own familiar friend, and yet
   By chance I found her
Half hidden in a dusty tray,
'Mid tawdry trinkets of to-day,
While draggled stores of cast array
   Hung all around her.

Touched here and there with tarnished gold
Shines the small head, with tresses rolled
High in a knot of classic mould :
   Almost pathetic
The girlish profile seems to be—
Instinct with faith and purity
(Yet all surmise at most can be
   But theoretic).

I fain would think that, good and wise,
She viewed the world with steadfast eyes,
Stepping through life in modest guise,
    Beloved and cherished ;
But whether writ in gold or tears,
Or filled with homely hopes and fears,
Her story, with the withered years,
    Is past and perished.

Her eyes' soft colour no one knows,
Nor may this dusky slip disclose
If reigned the lily or the rose
    In her complexion ;
Yet sure unstinted praise should win
The parted lips, nor full, nor thin ;
The curved contours of throat and chin
    Are just—perfection.

I see her in the distance dim,
A white-gowned figure, straight and slim,
Fulfilling, free from doubt or whim,
    Her simple duty :

Who watched her in the square oak pew?
Who praised her cakes and elder-brew?
Who sent her valentines—and who
    Decried her beauty?

Maybe in some old secrétaire
A faded ringlet of her hair,
Or sampler stitched with patient care
    By her deft fingers,
Or faint pot-pourri in a bowl
Bedecked with gay festoon and scroll
(Fit relic of so sweet a soul!)
    Forgotten lingers.

No longer jingles her spinet
To madrigal or minuet,
But, dumb with mildew and regret,
    And all asthmatic,
Forgetful now of tune and tone,
With hoary cobwebs overgrown,
And (save for nesting mice) alone,
    Stands in an attic.

Our world is full of broken toys;
Some baser leaven oft alloys
The fame that claims with certain voice
  A sure remembrance;
But she—we see her at her best,
A maiden wiser than the rest
In leaving, as her sole bequest,
  So fair a semblance.

SPRING SONG

So few and sweet,
The pale spring days draw near with timid feet—
Draw near and pass, alas! in swift retreat,
So few and sweet!

So few and sweet
Do dark wet violets our senses greet,
Where faint red sun-rays on the mosses meet,
So few and sweet!

So sweet and few
Those meadow-memories all dim with dew,
The veil withdrawn at dawn, with glimpses through
So sweet and few!

So sweet and few!
More sweet than all the roses June may strew;
Love, of Remembrance, weeping, born anew,
Bewails those hours the after-season slew,
So sweet and few!

SCYTHE SONG

(August 1887. *Longman's Magazine.*)

STALWART mowers, brown and lithe,
  Over summer meads abloom,
Wielding fast the whispering Scythe,
  Where is all the old perfume?
Breathes it yet in tender gloom,
  Soft through Hades' twilight air?
Where hath Summer-tide her tomb?
  Hush! the Scythe says, *where, ah where?*

Comes the long blade, gleaming cold,
  Where the garden-ground is spread—
Rays of pearl on crowns of gold,
  Dainty daisies, white and red!
Dames that o'er them once would tread,
  Damsels blithe and debonair,
Where is all your sweetness fled?
  Hush! the Scythe says, *where, ah where?*

Time ! who tak'st and giv'st again
  All things bitter, some things sweet,
Must we follow, all in vain .
  Follow still those phantom feet?
Is there not some grass-grown street,
  Some old, yew-begirt parterre,
Where our Dreams and we may meet?
  Hush ! the Scythe says, *where, ah where ?*

FLEUR-DE-LYS

By the path, on either hand,
   Rising from the garden-bed,
Stately lilies once would stand,
   Once would tower above my head ;
   Hardly reached 'twixt joy and dread,
Held by straining finger-tips,
   These their shower of gold would shed
(Fairy gold !) upon my lips.

Gay is yet the garden-plot,
   Rich in gold and ivory,
Lilies fresh and fine, but not—
   Not the buds that used to be.
   These are white and fair to see,
These to-day I bend above ;
   Those were Queens that stooped to me
In their languor and their love.

PETITE CHANSON PICARDE

PALE leaves waver and whisper low
  (Silvered leaves of the poplar tree),
Waters wander and willows blow
           In Picardie.

Misty green of the orchard grass,
  Grass-grown lanes by the sedge-fringed lea,
Pleasant ways for the feet that pass
           Through Picardie.

Here the youth on a blue May night
  Soft to his maiden's home steals he,
Binds a bough to the lintel's height
           Of dark fir tree.

Gaston sigheth for Bernadette!
  (Sorrow to come—or joy to be?)
This she knows by the token set
           In secrecy.

Long lagoons where the lilies lie
  (Blossoms and buds of ivory),
Sweet the meadows and fair the sky
            Of Picardie!

Where be the waters to drown regret?
  Where be the leaves of Sleep's own tree?
Nowhere else in the world—nor yet
            In Picardie.

LES BREBIS DU PÈRE JACQUES

ON a rainy autumn day
    There is shelter under the eaves
For brown birds slim and gay,
    And under the broad vine-leaves.

They cling on the old white wall,
    And swing in the wet green vine,
Twittering, one and all,
    Of play in the past sunshine.

The house is so still to-day—
    Only the rustle and cheep
Of small brown birds at play:
    For the owner lies asleep.

He saw through his window-pane,
    As the autumn dawn uprose
Grey through the dripping rain,
    Dim green of an orchard-close.

He said, ' But the fold is far,
    And the sun is hid to-day ;
And I know not where they are—
    My sheep that have gone astray.

' Yet I hear their pattering feet,
    And I feel the dust-cloud rise ;
They are following down the street,
    And the dust-cloud dims mine eyes.'

Still the warm rain pattered on
    With its sound of flocks that sped,
Till a misty sun-shaft shone
    On an old man lying dead.

The little white house is still ;
    But the rain sings soft and clear,
The small birds twitter shrill,
    And the dead man smiles to hear.

BYGONES

THE moon swings low on the twilight,
   A glory of tawny gold,
And I would she might give me tidings
   Of my comrades known of old,
When, kissed by the sun and the sea-winds,
   Here a garden once would be,
A garden among the pine-trees,
   And a child that laughed with me.

Gone are the pines and their plumage,
   Gone is the gold-haired child,
And all that is left of the garden
   Is a red-rose tree run wild :
Winged like the wavering sea-birds,
   Flitting from shore to shore,
The pine-trees stray unresting ;
   The child is a child no more.

We know not either of other,
  Nor aught of the time between ;
But the wind blowing up from the sand-dunes
  Hath heard, and the moon hath seen :
They are mute, being loth to grieve us,
  Who watched when we both were gay ;
I who am I no longer,
  They that no more aré they.

A PASTORAL

(*IN MONOTONE*)

TO B. L.

LONG misty lines sweep downward to the bay,
White sea-birds waver by, and dull sheep stray
   Pale on the low, brown bosom of the hill ;
Wan twilight hangs her veil in skies of grey.

On the field's slope, laid light against the sky,
Thin, withered stems, their frail hands lifting high,
   Implore to look upon dead Summer's face,
One tender moment, as they waste and die.

Small, creeping waves wash whispering on the sand,
Low writhen tamarisks, leaning from the strand,
   With branches spread beneath the wild wind's will,
Sway, softly beckoning between sea and land.

The winter evening breathes completest rest :
(Intenser thrills of sunset leave the West
   Disconsolate, and thronged with memories.)
When storm-winds sleep, low tones—grey skies—are
    best.

G

EVENING

TO A. G. L.

'The sound of a sea without wind is about them, and sunset is red.'

THE wild gulls wheel and waver,
   They call and cry,
In sad, shrill notes that quaver
   'Tween earth and sky :
The red sun sinks apace,
While yet his gleaming face
Looks out a moment's space
   Through mists that fly.

The toiling team move slowly
   In rhythmic beat,
With patient heads bent lowly,
   Their heavy feet
Past fresh-cut furrows clear ;
While low waves whisper near,
And sweet earth-odours here
   The salt airs meet.

Dim wings of twilight hover
  O'er field and sea,
For day is past and over ;
  And silently,
With weary sense and sight,
Through veils of fading light,
The ploughman welcomes night
  Where rest shall be.

A WAYSIDE CALVARY

THE carven Christ hangs gaunt and grim
  Beneath his blue Picardian skies,
And piteous, perchance, to him
  Seems every man that lives and dies.
  Here, hid from hate of alien eyes,
Two hundred Prussians sleep, they say,
  Beneath the cross whose shadow lies
Athwart the road to Catelet.

'Mid foes they slumber unafraid,
  Made whole by Death, the cunning leech,
Anear the long white roadway laid
  By his cold arms, beyond all reach
  Of *Heimweh* pangs or stranger's speech :
Of curse or blessing naught reck they,
  Of snows that hide nor suns that bleach
The dusty road to Catelet.

Of garlands laid or blossoms spread
  The Prussians' sun-scorched mound lies bare ;
But thin grass creeps above the dead,
  And pallid poppies flutter fair,
  And fling their drowsy treasures there
Beneath the symbol, stark and grey,
  That hath the strangers in its care
Beside the road to Catelet.

THE QUICK AND THE DEAD

UNDER the grass and the graveyard clay
   Faint fall the voices from overhead.
   Rough is the road for the quick to tread.
Breasting the tide and the tempest they—
Mine is the haven of life's heyday.
   They are dying, but I am dead !

Oh, but the daisies and long grass under,
   I, with my myriad lives instead,
Listening, laughing, I hear them wonder—
   They are dying, but I am dead !

I, with my myriad lives again,
Grass and roses, and leaves and rain,
They with their struggle with doubt and pain,
They with the strangling throes to come,
   They with the grip of the grave to dread.
God ! how I laugh in my quiet home—
   They are dying, but I am dead !

Oh ! but the life of me ! gathering, growing,
    Emmet and butterfly, flower and thorn,
Poppy and rose in the gold sun glowing,
    Over and over unmade, re-born.

One with the grey of the winter day,
    One with the glint of the sunset gold,
One with the wind and the salt sea-spray,
    One with the dun of the furrowed mould.

How shall I joy in the world unwitting ?
    How shall I lean to the dear warm sun ?
Grub or nightingale—creeping or flitting—
    Nature and I in the end made one.

Only the life of me one with thee :
    Body and soul of us joined and wed.
Shall we not pity them, I and she,
    They the dying and we the dead ?

ON THE ROAD

THE snow is white, the way is stern and sore,
Wide, blinding wastes behind us and before,
And though we soon shall see a stiller shore,
    The road is long.

The gaunt grey wolves are famished for their prey,
But we are bound, and hungrier than they ;
The fruit will fall when we ourselves are clay—
    The road is long.

We leave strong hands to cleanse away the stain,
Though we plod on along the shuddering plain
To marching music of the creaking chain—
    The road is long.

The sands of Tyranny are slow to run.
Alas ! that this and many a morrow's sun
Must see the goal ungained, the work undone !
    The road is long.

Our lives were ladder-rungs : the Cause moves on ;
The light shines fair as ever it has shone ;
'Twill blaze full bright ere many years be gone—
    The road is long.

We are but bubbles breaking in the sea,
The strong slow tide that one day will be free ;
We shall not know it—yea, but it will be :
    The road is long.

HYMN OF LABOUR

' WOE for the bale and the burden, the weary wasting
    of days!
Woe for the toil and the tangle, the dim desolation
    of ways!
Lost, in mist of the Past, are the early faiths and
    fears;
Dead, in the womb of the Future, the dream of the
    distant years.
Shadows lengthen and shrink, and bleak day followeth
    day;
Idle are all words spoken—What is there left to
    say?'

This—it is well, indeed, that the old faiths slumber
    and sleep;
This—that the dream deemed dead may one day
    quicken and leap:

Winter is well forgotten, but Spring and Summer for
  toil—
Go, turn thy feet to the fields for birth of the corn
  and oil!
Leave thy wreck of the Future—thy grave of a dead
  delight;
Lift hard hands to the plough, and gird strong loins
  for the fight.

Strive for the strife's sake only, smite not foeman nor
  friend—
Strive for the strife's sake only, set no shrine for an
  end;
Set no goal for the winning, no bright bourne for the
  scope;
Ask no guerdon of praise, and hope thou nothing
  from Hope.
If, afar in the sunrise, white wings flash and are fled,
Lift not thy hand from the toiling, turn not aside
  thine head.

Corn-husks gladden the swine, and ashes are left of
  fire,
Dead leaves shake on the trees—but what thing comes
  of Desire?

Dear is the Peace after Pain, and balm for the flint-
  worn feet ;
Great peace cometh of Labour—out of the Strong
  the Sweet.

So shalt thou come to thy reaping, so shalt thou say
  —it is well—
With lips redeemed from the curse, and soul from the
  uttermost hell.
So shalt thou look through the sunset, glad, and
  weary, and free,
Saying, 'A little space only—a little while—but I
  see.'

THE SMILE OF ALL-WISDOM

SEEKING the Smile of All-Wisdom one wandered
    afar
  (He that first fashioned the Sphinx, in the dusk of
    the past) :
Looked on the faces of sages, of heroes of war ;
Looked on the lips of the lords of the uttermost star,
    Magi, and kings of the earth—nor had found it at
    last,

Save for the word of a slave, hoary-headed and weak,
    Trembling, that clung to the hem of his garment,
    and said,
'Master, the least of your servants has found what
    you seek :
  (Pardon, O Master, if all without wisdom I speak !)
*Sculpture the smile of your Sphinx from the lips of the
    Dead !'*

Rising, he followed the slave to a hovel anear ;
  Lifted the mat from the doorway and looked on the
    bed.
' Nay, thou hast spoken aright, thou hast nothing to
    fear :
That which I sought thou hast found, Friend ; for, lo,
    it is here !—
  Surely the Smile of the Sphinx is the Smile of the
    Dead ! '

Aye, on the stone lips of old, on the clay of to-day,
  Tranquil, inscrutable, sweet with a quiet disdain,
Lingers the Smile of All-Wisdom, still seeming to
    say,
' Fret not, O Friend, at the turmoil—it passeth away ;
  Waste not the Now in the search of a Then that is
    vain :

' Hushed in the infinite dusk at the end shall ye be,
  Feverish, questioning spirits that travail and yearn,
Quenched in the fulness of knowledge and peaceful
    as we :
Lo, we have lifted the veil—there was nothing to see !
  Lo, we have looked on the scroll—there was nothing
    to learn ! '

'ELI, ELI, LAMA SABACHTHANI?'

STRAIGHT, slender limbs strained stark upon the cross,
  Dim, anguished eyes that search the empty sky,—
All human loneliness, and pain, and loss,
  Brake forth in thine exceeding bitter cry,
Thou King of Martyrs, lifted up on high
  For men to mock at in thine agony :
Would that that last, worst cup had passed thee by !
  Would that thy God had not forsaken Thee !

The cry of each man born that loves or prays—
  Yea, be his idol human or divine,
Body or soul sinks dead in thorny ways
  Before the marsh-lit lantern of a shrine :
I, Friend, have my God—ay, and thou hast thine ;
  Art, Fortune, Pleasure, Love? or Christ, may be ?
Shall the cry rise from thy lips first ? or mine ?
  ' Why hast thou, O my God, forsaken me ? '

A weak soul wailing in the body's slough ;
  A strong man bent beneath a leaden Fate;
Dead hopes, crushed toys, and shattered gods !—O
    Thou
  Whom high desires and dreams left desolate,
We cannot tread Thy narrow path and strait
  But all our pity and love go forth to Thee—
Thine is the cry of each soul soon or late :
  'Why hast thou, O my God, forsaken me ?'

Grief is, and was, and evermore must be,
  Even as long waves, gathering again,
Moan to and fro between the shore and sea ;
  And, as the wind wails blindly through the rain,
So all earth-voices echo—aye in vain—
  The ceaseless questioning and piteous,
The old appeal against eternal pain :
  'Why hast thou, O our God, forsaken us?'

TRANSLATIONS

H

OLD BOOKS, FRESH FLOWERS

(*TRANSLATED FROM THE FRENCH OF JOSEPH BOULMIER*)

ALONE, at home, I dwell, content and free :
 The soft May sun comes with his greeting fair ;
And, like a lute, my heart thrills tremblingly,
 By the Spring's fingers touched to some sweet air.
Blessed be Thou, my God, who from my face
 Tak'st the pale cast of thought that weary lowers !
My chamber walls—my narrow window-space
 Hold all most dear to me—old books, fresh flowers.

Those trusty friends, that faithful company—
 My books—say, 'Long his slumbers, and we wait !'
But my flowers murmur as they look on me,
 'Nay, never chide him, for he watched so late !'
Brethren and sisters, these of mine ! my room
 Shines fair as with the light of Eden's bowers ;
The Louvre is not worth my walls abloom
 With all most dear to me—old books, fresh flowers.

H 2

Beside your shelves I know not weariness,
  My silent-speaking books! so kind and wise ;
And fairer seems your yellowed parchment dress
  Than gay morocco, to my loving eyes.
Dear blossoms, of the humble hermit's choice,
  In sweetest communing what joys are ours!
To you I listen, and with you rejoice ;
  For all I love is here—old books, fresh flowers.

Men are unlovely, but their works are fair—
  Ay, men are evil, but their books are good :
The clay hath perished, and the soul laid bare
  Shines from their books in heavenly solitude.
Light on each slender stem pure blossoms rest,
  Like angel envoys of the Heavenly powers ;
Of all earth's maidens these are first and best,
  And all I love is here—old books, fresh flowers.

A double harvest crowns my granary :
  From all light loves and joys my soul takes flight ;
My books are blossoms, and their bee am I,
  And God's own volumes are my blossoms bright.

These and no other bosom-friends are mine ;
    With them I pass my best, my calmest hours ;
These only lead me to the light Divine,
    And all I love is here : old books, fresh flowers.

My books are tombs where wit and wisdom sleep,
    Stored full with treasure of the long ago ;
My tender buds, that dews of springtide steep,
    Like shining mirrors of the future show.
The present is so sad ! . . . . this dark to-day
    Like skies with thunder charged above us lowers :
Ah ! of the past—the future—speak alway,
    Tell me of naught but these . . . . old books, fresh
        flowers.

THE BROIDERED BODICE

(OLD FRENCH)

1600

'DEAR MY LOVE, I must ride away,
Fare ye well for a summer's day;
   Loth am I to leave your side,
   Yet your lover to Nantes must ride,
For the king commands and I obey.'

'Now, in sooth, if to Nantes ye fare,
Thence, I pray you, a bodice bear—
   Broidery-work on the breast and sleeves,
   Of roses white with silvery leaves,
Silvery roses white and fair.'

Now to Nantes hath her gallant gone,
But never the bodice thought upon;
   Filled his thoughts with the wine and play,
   Making merry the livelong day—
All the day till the torches shone.

' But what shall I say to my ladye,
Who a broidered bodice prayed of me?'
   ' Speak her soft and speak her smooth,
   Say, "Through Nantes I searched, in truth,
And none such bodices there might be."'

' Better a sea where no fish are,
Better the night without a star,
   Hills with never a valley set,
   Spring with never a violet,
Sweeter were all these things to me
Than a lying speech to my ladye.'

A BALLAD

(FROM THE ITALIAN)

MY steps have trod the fiery halls of Hell,
  Yea, even mine, and are retraced again.
Mother of Grace! how many there do dwell!
  And there my love these many days hath lain.
She sprang to greet me swiftly, joyfully :
  ' Dear heart,' she cried, ' dost thou remember not
Those days when " Sweet my soul " thou calledst me ?
  Still do I crave thy kisses unforgot,
Still weep the summers dead when I was thine.
  Let but thy lips assuage my lips that yearn !
So sweet thy mouth, of pity sweeten mine !
  Lo, thou hast kissed me ! hope not to return.'

THE AUBADE

(OLD FRENCH FOLK-SONG)

IT is the lads of Longpré, so light of heart and gay,
And they are gone to Wanel, their sweet aubade to
    play :
And from his house the maréchal looks forth at break
    of day,
Says, 'Tell me for what lady's sake your sweet aubade
    you play ?
Come tell me, lads of Longpré, for whom you sing ? '
    saith he.
' Now, peace be with you, maréchal, 'tis not for your
    ladye ;
'Tis all for your good neighbour's lass, who bideth
    you anear.'
(Now well the maid might hearken, so brave they
    spoke and clear !)
And up she rose, the neighbour's lass, did on her
    linen gown,
She took the pitcher in her hand and to the stream
    went down.

'Now why go ye so heavily, now why so pale art
seen ?
Whence come ye, whither go ye, O maiden sad of
mien ? '
'Nay, well may I go heavily, and well be sad of
mien,
Since I, of all my lovers, have nought but woe and
teen ;
For one is hanged, and one is burned, another waits
the death,
Another, at the king's fair court, the torture suffereth ;
Yes—one is hanged, and one is burned, the others
fear the fire,—
And one lives aye within my heart ; he is my heart's
desire.'

NEW WORDS TO OLD TUNES

THE BOURNE

'WHAT goal remains for pilgrim feet,
  Now all our gods are banished?'
Afar, where sea and sunrise meet,
  Tall portals bathed in gold and red,
  From either door a carven head
Smiles down on men full drowsily
  'Mid mystic forms of wings outspread
Between the Gates of Ivorie.

Now if beyond lie town or street
  I know not, nor hath any said,
Though tongues wag fast and winds are fleet:
  Some say that there men meet the dead,
  Or filmy phantoms in their stead,
And some, 'It leads to Arcadie.'
  In sooth, I know not, yet would tread
Between the Gates of Ivorie.

For surely there sounds music sweet,
  With fair delights and perfumes shed,
And all things broken made complete,
  And found again things forfeited ;
  All this for him who scorning dread
Shall read the wreathen fantasie,
  And pass, where no base soul hath sped,
Between the Gates of Ivorie.

Ah, Princess ! grasp the golden thread,
  Rise up and follow fearlessly,
By high desire and longing led
  Between the Gates of Ivorie.

DEAD POETS

WHERE be they that once would sing,
   Poets passed from wood and dale?
Faintly, now, we touch the string,
   Faithless, now, we seek the Grail :
   Shakspeare, Spenser, nought avail,
Herrick, England's Oberon,
   Sidney, smitten through his mail,
Souls of Poets dead and gone!

Ronsard's Roses blossoming
   Long are faded, long are frail;
Gathered to the heart of Spring
   He that sang the breezy flail.[1]
   Ah! could prayer at all prevail,
These should shine where once they shone,
   These should 'scape the shadowy pale—
Souls of Poets dead and gone!

[1] Joachim du Bellay.

What clear air knows Dante's wing ?
  What new seas doth Homer sail ?
By what waters wandering
  Tells Theocritus his tale ?
  Still, when cries the Nightingale, ·
Singing, sobbing, on and on,
  Her brown feathers seem to veil
Souls of Poets dead and gone !

Charon, when my ghost doth hail
  O'er Cocytus' waters wan,
Land me where no storms assail
  Souls of Poets dead and gone.

THE MARSH OF ACHERON

BETWEEN the Midnight and the Morn,
  The under-world my soul espied ;
I saw the shades of men outworn,
  The Heroes fallen in their pride ;
    I saw the marsh-lands drear and wide,
And many a ghost that strayed thereon ;
  'Still must I roam,' a maiden sighed,
'The sunless marsh of Acheron.'

'And is thy fate thus hope-forlorn ? '
  'Yea, even so,' the shade replied,
'For one I wronged in life hath sworn
  In hatred ever to abide :
  The lover seeketh not the bride,
But aye, with me, his heart dreams on,
  Asleep in these cold mists that hide
The sunless marsh of Acheron.

I

'And still for me will Lacon mourn,
  And still my pardon be denied :
Ah, never shall I cross the bourne
  That Dead from Living doth divide.
  Yet I repent me not !' she cried,
'Nay—only that mine hour is gone ;
  One memory hath glorified
The sunless marsh of Acheron.'

Ah, Princess ! when *thy* ghost shall glide
  Where never star nor sunlight shone
See thou she tarry not beside
  The sunless marsh of Acheron.

ASPHODEL

Κατ' ἀσφοδελὸν λειμῶνα

NOW who will thread the winding way,
  Afar from fervid summer heat,
Beyond the sunshafts of the day,
  Beyond the blast of winter sleet?
  In the green twilight, dimly sweet,
Of poplar shades the shadows dwell,
  Who found erewhile a fair retreat
Along the mead of Asphodel.

There death and birth are one, they say;
  Those lowlands bear no yellow wheat
No sound doth rise of mortal fray,
  Of lowing herds, of flocks that bleat
  Nor wind nor rain doth blow nor beat;
Nor shrieketh sword, nor tolleth bell;
  But lovers one another greet
Along the mead of Asphodel.

I would that there my soul might stray ;
I would my phantom, fair and fleet,
Might cleave the burden of the clay,
Might leave the murmur of the street,
Nor with half-hearted prayer entreat
The half-believed-in Gods ; too well
I know the name I shall repeat
Along the mead of Asphodel.

Queen Proserpine, at whose white feet
In life my love I may not tell,
Wilt give me welcome when we meet
Along the mead of Asphodel ?

FAIRY GOLD.

A GOBLIN, trapped in netted skein,
  Did bruise his wings with vain essay;
' Now who will rend this hempen chain ?
  Let that man ask me what he may,
  I shall not, surely, say him nay :
The shadows wane, the day grows old ;
  Meseems this mesh will keep for aye
The sun-bright glint of Fairy Gold !'

These echoes of the creature's pain,
  As in the fowler's net he lay,
Drew soon anigh a surly swain,
  Who cut the cords and freed the fay :
  ' Now what fair gift shall well repay
Thy service done ?—for words are cold—
  Sweet looks or wisdom ? vine or bay ?'
' The sun-bright glint of Fairy Gold.'

'Thou choosest ill, but speech is vain ;
  Lo ! here is treasure good and gay : '
The goatherd grasped his golden gain
  And bore the shining store away ;
  He oped his chest, at break of day,
To find—no talents, bright and cold,
  But soft, dead cowslips—nowhere lay
The sun-bright glint of Fairy Gold !

Take hands, O Prince, for we will stray,
  We twain, where nought is bought or sold,
And find in every woodland way
  The sun-bright glint of Fairy Gold.

THE FLIGHT OF NICOLETE

ALL bathed in pearl and amber light
   She rose to fling the lattice wide,
And leaned into the fragrant night,
   Where brown birds sang of summertide
   ('Twas Love's own voice that called and cried).
'Ah, Sweet!' she said, 'I'll seek thee yet,
   Though thorniest pathways should betide
The fair white feet of Nicolete.'

They slept, who would have stayed her flight
   (Full fain were they the maid had died!)
She dropped adown her prison's height
   On strands of linen featly tied.
   And so she passed the garden-side,
With loose-leaved roses sweetly set,
   And dainty daisies, dark beside
The fair white feet of Nicolete!

Her lover lay in evil plight
  (So many lovers yet abide !)
I would my tongue could praise aright
  Her name, that should be glorified.
  Those lovers now, whom foes divide,
A little weep,—and soon forget.
  How far from these faint lovers glide
The fair white feet of Nicolete.

My Princess, doff thy frozen pride,
  Nor scorn to pay Love's golden debt ;
Through his dim woodland take for guide
  The fair white feet of Nicolete.

MIGHT BE

YOUNG Love flies fast, on wavering wing,
   Full fast he flies for woe or weal,
And some do bear his grievous sting
   Too deep for any leech to heal ;
   I scorn to swell their sad appeal,
False phantom, fled from our embrace !
   And yet—I doubt me I might kneel
Should you but chance to turn your face.

Of days long done our praises ring
   Right loud and full, a valorous peal,
For life was then a lusty thing :
   Ah ! then were mighty blows to deal.
   Brave days, my masters !—still, I feel
In sooth I could not deem him base
   Who'd shun your stare, O age of steel !
Should you but chance to turn your face.

'Alas !' our dainty minstrels sing,
  'That sorrow sets unbroken seal
On saint and sinner, clown and king.'
  They beg death's boon with busy zeal.
  They'll do you homage warm and leal,
Death ! while you pass their dwelling-place,
  But lips would gape and senses reel
Should you but chance to turn your face.

Queen Fortune of the mystic wheel,
  We bow to find you full of grace,
We would not turn on sullen heel
  Should *you* but chance to turn your face.

THE OPTIMIST

HEED not the folk who sing or say
   In sonnet sad or sermon chill,
'Alas! alack! and well-a-day!
   This round world's but a bitter pill!'
   Poor porcupines of fretful quill!
Sometimes we quarrel with our lot:
   We, too, are sad and careful—still,
We'd rather be alive than not.

What though we wish the cats at play
   Would some one else's garden till;
Though Sophonisba drop the tray
   And all our worshipped Worcester spill,
   Though neighbours 'practise' loud and shrill,
Though May be cold and June be hot,
   Though April freeze and August grill,—
We'd rather be alive than not.

And, sometimes, on a summer's day
  To self and every mortal ill
We give the slip, we steal away,
  To lie beside some sedgy rill ;
  The darkening years, the cares that kill,
A little while are well forgot ;
  Deep in the broom upon the hill
We'd rather be alive than not.

Pistol, with oaths didst thou fulfil
  The task thy braggart tongue begot.
We eat our leek with better will,
  We'd rather be alive than not.

BETTY BARNES, THE BOOK-BURNER

WHERE is that baleful maid
  Who Shakspeare's quartos shred?
Whose slow diurnal raid
  The flames with *Stephen* fed?
  Where is *Duke Humphrey* sped?
Where is the *Henries'* book?
  They all are vanishèd
With Betty Barnes the Cook.

And now her ghost, dismayed,
  In woful ways doth tread—
(Though once the grieving shade
  Sir Walter visited)—
  Where culprits sore bestead,
In dank or fiery nook,
  Repent their deeds of dread
With Betty Barnes the Cook.

There Bagford's evil trade
  Is duly punishèd ;
There fierce the flames have played
  Round Caliph Omar's head ;
  The biblioclastic dead
Have diverse pains to brook,
  'Mid rats and rainpools led
With Betty Barnes the Cook.

Caxton !   Be comforted,
  For those who wronged thee—look ;
They break affliction's bread
  With Betty Barnes the Cook.

MY ASTER PLATE [1]

My Aster plate hangs safe upon the wall
In rounded perfectness, nor large, nor small,
  No more 'mid yon swart Hebrew's wares to be ;
  I saw, I bought, I bore it joyfully
In hidden triumph from the huckster's stall.

The sun may hide his rolling golden ball,
The moon may sulk behind her purple pall,
  But thou art sun and moon and stars to me,
                My Aster plate !

Have mercy, Fortune, on thy trembling thrall !
And spare this dark blue disc, his all-in-all ;
  Wife, children, friends, I'll freely yield to thee,
  My books, my buhl, my much-loved marquetrie ;
Take these—but let no evil chance befall
                My Aster plate.

---

[1] Reprinted from the *Art Journal,* by permission of Messrs.
Virtue & Co.

TO HESPERUS

(AFTER BION)

O JEWEL of the deep blue night,
  Too soon, to-day, the moon arose ;
I pray thee, lend thy lovely light.

Than any other star more bright
  An hundredfold thy beauty glows,
O jewel of the deep blue night.

Too soon Selene gained the height,
  And now no more her glory shows ;
I pray thee, lend *thy* lovely light.

Anon our revel of delight
  Towards the shepherd's dwelling goes,
O jewel of the deep blue night !

And I must lead the dance aright,
  Yea—even I—for me they chose :
I pray thee, lend thy lovely light.

No thief am I, nor evil wight,
   Nor numbered with the traveller's foes,
O jewel of the deep blue night !

None would I spoil, nor e'en affright ;
   Mine are the Lover's joys and woes :
I pray thee, lend thy lovely light.

For good it is, in all men's sight
   (Thou knowest well), to favour those,
O jewel of the deep blue night !

Thy golden lamp hath turned to white
   The silver of the olive-close ;
O jewel of the deep blue night !
I pray thee, lend thy lovely light.

K

LOVE, THE GUEST

I DID not dream that Love would stay,
  I deemed him but a passing guest,
Yet here he lingers many a day.

I said, 'Young Love will flee with May
  And leave forlorn the hearth he blest,'
I did not dream that Love would stay.

My envious neighbour mocks me, 'Nay,
  Love lies not long in any nest.'
Yet here he lingers many a day.

And though I did his will alway,
  And gave him even of my best,
I did not dream that Love would stay.

I have no skill to bid him stay,
  Of tripping tongue or cunning jest,
Yet here he lingers many a day.

Beneath his ivory feet I lay
   Pale plumage of the ringdove's breast,
I did not dream that Love would stay.

Will Love be flown? I ofttimes say,
   Home turning for the noonday rest,
Yet here he lingers many a day.

His gold curls gleam, his lips are gay,
   His eyes through tears smile loveliest ;
I did not dream that Love would stay.

He sometimes sighs, when far away
   The low red sun makes fair the west,
Yet here he lingers many a day.

Thrice blest of all men am I ! yea,
   Although of all unworthiest ;
I did not dream that Love would stay,
Yet here he lingers many a day.

JEAN-FRANÇOIS MILLET

O MASTER of the Old and New!
  We speak thy name with bated breath ;
Thy waking years were all too few.

With airs that erst in Athens blew
  Thy toil's full harvest murmureth,
O Master of the Old and New!

In misty pastures, dim with dew,
  Thy sad, strong spirit slumbereth ;
Thy waking years were all too few.

The forms thy potent pencil drew
  On sunset light move strong as Death,
O Master of the Old and New!

The sowing seasons turn anew,
  And toiling man continueth ;
Thy waking years were all too few.

Dark Orcus veils thee from our view
  On vast, low meadow-lands of Death,
O Master of the Old and New.

Now men their tardy laurels strew,
  And Fame, remorseful, sobbing saith,
'O Master of the Old and New,
Thy waking years were all too few!'

OF HIMSELF

A POOR cicala, piping shrill,
   I may not ape the Nightingale ;
I sit upon the sun-browned hill,
A poor cicala, piping shrill,
When summer noon is warm and still,
   Content to chirp my homely tale ;
A poor cicala, piping shrill,
   I may not ape the Nightingale.

BLIND LOVE

LOVE hath wept till he is blind,
  Lovers, guide him on his way;
Though he be of fickle mind,
Love hath wept till he is blind.
Once ye knew him fair and kind;
  Now, alas and well-a-day!
Love hath wept till he is blind—
  Lovers, guide him on his way!

LES ROSES MORTES

THE roses are dead,
  And swallows are flying :
White, golden, and red,
The roses are dead ;
Yet tenderly tread
  Where their petals are lying :
The roses are dead,
  And swallows are flying.

PRINTED BY
SPOTTISWOODE AND CO., NEW-STREET SQUARE
LONDON